'Jolly Jack' Dunn

1923 - 2004

'Jolly Jack' Dunn

'Jolly Jack' Dunn
1923 - 2004
an illustrated history of his life

Edited by Peter Gripton from Jack Dunn's original recollections

Copyright © Peter Gripton 2006

First Published 2006 by kenandglen.com
Second Edition 2007 Las Atalayas Publishing

The moral rights of the author have been asserted. all rights reserved. No part of this publication may be reproduced, stored in a retrieval system or transmitted in any form or by any means, electronic, mechanical or ortherwise without the written permssion of the Publisher.

ISBN 978-0-9556753-5-5

'Jolly Jack' Dunn

'Jolly Jack' Dunn

'Jolly Jack' Dunn

Editor's note:

I'd just returned from a summer holiday in Cornwall on the last day of July (2004) and been sent to replenish stocks at the local supermarket, when I happened to spot Brenda Dunn, along with her daughter Jennifer. I must confess that I hadn't seen Jennifer for a number of years, probably not since I worked in *'The Silver Birch'* during the early Seventies. I started to make some joking comment about something or other, but the look on Brenda's face stopped me in my tracks. *"I'm afraid I've got some bad news, Pete"*, she said, then told me that her husband Jack had died just a few days previously. Jack hadn't been very well for quite some time but, whenever I had dropped in to see him, there had always been a warm welcome, usually accompanied by many a quip or joke. Thus it was that on Friday 6th August, along with a **Greatham Church** full of mourners, I sat and listened to some of the many tributes paid to Jack, during his funeral service.

Huguette Jenkinson, a lay-reader in her own right, officiated at the service and gave some flavour of the man; this was later added to, firstly by Simon Sillence, an old friend of Jack's from the local Royal Naval Association (RNA), and then, movingly, by his grandson David. Simon's eulogy was later reproduced on the front page of an issue of the local RNA newsletter, *'Up Spirits'*, and is given in full below:

"We are here to celebrate the life of Jack Dunn, the Jolly Sailor. I first saw Jack one evening at the 'Jolly Sailor' pub in Petersfield, sometime in the 1970s – not in person, but his image was painted on the pub's signboard. Unbeknown to me, I would later see the man in person, as he served at the meat counter in the Gateway supermarket. His ready smile, wit and charm won over many a young mother and her toddlers, as he became known as the 'Jolly Butcher'.

Jack had joined the Navy at the age of seventeen years, not long after the outbreak of World War II. He trained at Whale Island in Pompey, first as a gunnery rating, then later as a 'hard hat' diver. This was a job that involved a great deal of danger, a physically and mentally demanding job, one that took courage and tenacity to do, often in total darkness, in cold and inhospitable waters.

He touched the lives of many of us, as those gathered here today can testify. One such event was Jack's diving, in great secrecy, on the wreck of the battleship 'Royal Oak', sunk by Kapitan Prien of U-boat U47 at Scapa Flow, with the loss of many lives. Among them was the brother of Ivy Howard, one of the congregation here today.

In the Pacific, on board the aircraft carrier 'Formidable', Jack survived kamikaze attacks by Japanese aircraft, intent on sinking his ship. In the same theatre of war, in a sister carrier 'Indomitable', he served alongside shipmate Malcolm Meech, another here today.

At the formation of the Liss and District Branch of the RNA, Jack and Brenda were among the founder members, along with Tommy and Ivy Howard, Malcolm and Jean Meech – their lives intertwined by their service to the Crown and the Royal Navy.

'Jolly Jack' Dunn

Jack always referred to me as 'Deeps', an affectionate nickname between fellow divers. We at Liss are proud and humbled to have known our shipmate Jack. The world is a little sadder for the 'crossing of the bar' of a sailor's sailor but, above all, we will remember Jack Dunn as the 'Jolly Sailor'".

Simon later kindly gave me permission to use the eulogy above, for which I am most grateful. I also reproduce grandson David's words below:

"*My grandfather, Jack Dunn, was born in 1923 in the North East but, in 1925, Jack's father, a Royal Engineer, was posted to Bordon and the family moved to* **Greatham**. *When Jack was in his late teens, he had a conversation with his father, during which his father called him 'a chicken' and told him that, "You want to get yourself some of these", pointing to his medals. During the course of the next week, Jack lied about his age and joined the Navy - he wasn't going to have anybody call him a chicken. He told me later in life that the reason he joined the Navy, rather than the Army, was that he didn't want to be "stuck down a foxhole". Jack progressed to being a gun trainer and Navy diver during the war. His most remarkable memory was of serving with the "forgotten fleet" in the Pacific, with the horrific experience of attack by Japanese 'Kamikaze' planes.*

To illustrate the type of man Jack was, one of Jack's shipmates was killed in action. Whilst firing the gun, to try and down the plane before it hit the ship, he had pushed his two colleagues off the gun, forfeiting his own life and saving the life of his mates. Jack saw all this and decided that, when he got back home, he would get in touch with his shipmate's family and tell them how much of a hero he had been. But Jack couldn't find out where they lived after the war. Astonishingly, some sixty years later, he found them living in Oldham in Lancashire. Unbeknown to Jack, his shipmate's wife had a baby boy while they were away, who had never seen his father. Jack was, at last, able to tell his shipmate's son how much of a hero his father was, for which the family was most grateful.

I use this story to illustrate the type of man Jack was - a happy, jolly man, always thinking of other people rather than himself. In fact, he was such a jolly man that, for a good few years, his face was that of the 'Jolly Sailor' pub sign, just outside of Petersfield. I can honestly say that Jack was still cracking his jokes, right up until the end. In the hospital, a very sincere lady doctor looked at Jack and asked, "Is there anything else I can do for you, Mr Dunn?" To which, only Jack could reply, "Yes, what are you doing Monday night?"

Brenda and Jack have had a very happy sixty-two years together, and Nan says she would change absolutely nothing about their years together. I will remember my Grandad as a very happy jolly man, who would do anything for anybody."

After the funeral service, I approached David and made myself known to him. Although living 'up north' himself, he promised me that he would let me have a copy of his tribute in due course – the result of which is shown above. David then told me that his grandfather had been 'something of a poet' and that he would, at some point in the future, like to publish Jack's works, which also included a brief historical account of his own life in the Navy. David must have worked hard on transcribing Jack's written account into computer format, which he would then dispatch to me, part by part, via that wonder of modern science – 'E-mail'. I eventually received this account in full and I am sure Jack would not have minded me doing some editing to turn it into the *'Life of Jack'* that now follows.

Peter Gripton, 2005

'Jolly Jack' Dunn

'Jolly Jack' Dunn

The life of Jack

My early days

My first recollection of life was as a small child, living in Army quarters. My father had come to Longmoor Camp, in Hampshire, to help build the Longmoor Military Railway, sometime in the nineteen-twenties. Dad (Thomas Dunn) had first served with the Lancashire Fusiliers in the Dardanelles during the First World War, where he was injured and presumed dead. Thus it came about that his name appears on the War Memorial up in Salford. So whenever we went to Salford, now part of Greater Manchester, he would proudly show me his name on the Memorial. As he put it, *"He was dead, but he wouldn't lie down"*. When he came back from Gallipoli, he transferred to the Royal Engineers at Catterick Camp (North Yorkshire), where he met my mother, who herself hailed from 'Geordieland', some distance further north.

Mother came from a miner's family of two daughters and five brothers and we used to go up north on visits every Christmas. There were always funerals taking place of men from the local 'pit' – or coalmine. That was a dangerous mine, it was a mile deep and extended some four miles out under the sea. The haulage of the coal tubs was all done by pit ponies. One of my uncles even reckoned he used to drive his ponies in his sleep - the language could be quite educational at times! The miners used to get a coal allowance of about half a ton a month. Young boys used to run after the coal lorry and ask the lady of the house if they could put the load through the hatch. If they had any luck, they would get anything from a threepenny bit to a 'tanner' (sixpence), but that included washing down the cobbles afterwards. The lads sometimes used to run as far as a mile after the lorry to get there first.

Jack's Dad Tommy Dunn, Jacks Uncle Tom, Jacks Grandad John
Jack's Mum Jane, Jacks Aunt Deb, Jacks Gran Eleanor

It was a hard life those days in Durham. On a Saturday, I used to go to draw my Grandad's pay for his six shifts – for six days a week he used to get just two pounds and six shillings for being a face worker, laid on his side with a huge shovel, loading coal onto a belt. When the Colliery football team was playing, the miners were always very keen to hear the results. So the men working on the cages, sending the tubs down the different seams, used to chalk the score on the side of the tubs. This way the seam workers used to get the score in only a few minutes. Their other favourite sports were 'the greyhounds' and darts. They also had their allotments, where they grew their famous leeks and onions for the local shows. Oh yes, and they were also great pigeon-fanciers.

Anyway, back to Longmoor! When I started my education, it was at the Infants' School, run by the Army, up in the Camp. We had an Army nurse in those days, who used to look after our ailments. The kids used to worship her - indeed, I have seen kids cut themselves so that they could be treated by Sister Phillips. Sadly, she went off on holiday, cut her foot and caught septicaemia, which killed her. All the schoolchildren walked down the road from Longmoor to **Greatham** after the hearse.

Whenever we got any infection as kids, they used to put a notice on your door, *'Keep out – infection'*, while Dad had to go off and sleep in the barracks. We all caught measles so, of course, we had the notice posted on the door. Dad wasn't allowed in the house, but he used to climb through the window and bring us cigarette cards and get his 'NAAFI break'. On one such day, my mother looked out of the window and spotted the Army doctor coming towards our house. She shouted to my Dad, *"Tom, here comes the doctor"*. Dad immediately jumped into the wardrobe and shut the door behind him. My brother and I were laid in bed and in came the doctor to look at us. After checking us over, he then asked, *"How is your Dad?"* My brother then replied, *"You can ask him yourself, he is in the wardrobe"* - and there stood my Dad with his arm slung up at the salute, it was so funny!

My Dad was put on a charge for that and confined to barracks, so we didn't get any fag cards for a week. It's a wonder my brother wasn't strangled! He was the terror of the Camp. He joined the local troop of 'Cubs' and they used to show him how to build a campfire. The following day he built his own campfire on the moors - and burned down over a hundred trees! My Dad was once again on a charge after that escapade. Then, just a week later, the doctor was looking at a child in a pram. My brother had picked up a piece of wood from the NAAFI, with a nail in it, and promptly belted the doctor's backside. The nail sank in and the doctor must have cleared the pram. So poor Dad was placed on a charge yet again. Another week we lost my brother, I think at the time he was only about five years old. They found him walking across the top spar of one of the rail bridges, some thirty feet above the ground. Needless to say, Dad was on yet another charge for that.

I left the Infant School for the older school, which was then being run by Sergeant Faber of the Education Corps, he was a good schoolmaster. An occasion that sticks in my mind was the day that *'HMS Queen Mary'* was launched - that must have been at

Tommy Dunn Senior and Junior at Longmoor, School Sports Day

Southampton. The teacher had the wireless going, so that we could all listen in to the event and, as they broke the cable, I managed to knock a vase of flowers off the table. So, as the *Queen Mary* was launched, I had five whacks across my rear, which certainly made me remember it! My dad sent me down to the stables of the Royal Horse Artillery (RHA) to see Paddy Kennedy for a hair cut. They sat me on a form and give me a cut with the horse shears! When I got home, my mum went spare as I hadn't a hair left on my head. I had to get permission to wear a cap in school.

When we got to the age of ten years, we then had to transfer to **Greatham School** down in the village. I think it was called a Council School in those days, with Mr Charles Wain being the headmaster. Just before that, I'd been a member of the choir at St Martin's Church, which had once been a forage barn for the RHA. The Padre at the time went by the name of Reverend Carter, he was not very well liked by the Army lads. This day in question was very cold and it was very hard to keep warm. So when he got up in the pulpit, he asked if the troops could put *"a little extra"* in the collection bags, to warm the Church. Now it was my job to collect the bags from the soldiers and so, the following Sunday, I went down the aisle with the brass offertory plate to collect the bags. Normally, I could guess by the weight whether we had a good collection or not. This particular week, the bags seemed very light.

My next job was to take the collection into the vestry and count it out into piles of coppers. There was never a lot of silver, as the troops didn't get much a week. *(My own father, with two kids to feed, only got thirty bob a week, that's just £1:50 in today's money.)* When I tipped the bags out I nearly died. To keep the church warm, as requested, they had all brought a small piece of coal each! I just got out quickly, as the Padre went mad. He certainly 'gave them some stick' the following week! I used to go down the NAAFI at the weekend and draw four loaves and a joint of meat for the family. If you gave the Army butcher a 'tip' of sixpence, you usually got a nice joint, but if not, then it was a job to chew it!

Reaching the age of fourteen, I had to leave school and get my first job, which was a paper round, covering the Empshott and Selborne area. I started at 6.30 each morning and usually finished about 1 p.m. The bike I used had no brakes, so it was a wonder I didn't get killed. I stuck to it for just a year, as I was always getting wet through, while my wage was only fifteen shillings (75p) a week. I then started working for the NAAFI, as errand boy. I used to deliver the paraffin in an old pram, it was a hard job.

(The term 'NAAFI' referred to above stands for Navy, Army and Air Force Institute, an organisation set up for the benefit of the Armed Forces, providing canteen and shopping facilities on a world-wide basis.)

A life on (and under) the ocean wave

It was definitely due to my father, who was then serving in the Royal Engineers, or 'Sappers', that I gained entry into the Navy. He had wanted me to join his own Regiment but, after being a kid in Army Quarters for nearly fourteen years, I was already pretty well 'cheesed off' with the Army. And I didn't fancy skulking in a trench or a foxhole! The Second World War had started and he told me I was too yellow to join 'the mob'. *(The mob is a slang term for Army. Ed.)* That did it! I was already seventeen years old, so off I went down to Portsmouth to join the Navy. I was met at Victoria Hall by a Chief Petty Officer (CPO), whose first question was, *"What do you want son?"* To which my reply was, *"I want to join the Navy"*. *"When do you want to start?"* he then asked. My answer was instant - *"Next week"*. He gave a large grin and said, *"Make it a fortnight!"*

Along with many other volunteers, I then stripped off, there were all shapes and sizes. *"Bend over, okay son, your hat is on straight"*. Then we were given little bottles for urine tests and we all stood in a row, over a line of sandbags, it was very humorous. Some of the lads had been for a drink before the medical so, when they started filling their bottles, they couldn't stop. So **that** was obviously the reason for the sandbags! On returning back home, my father barked at me, *"Why haven't you been at work?"* My reply was, *"Dad, you told me I was too yellow to join up, so I start at HMS Collingwood in two weeks time"*. My mother just about took off, she was a Geordie lass from Durham. She said to my Dad, in her broad Geordie accent, *"If aught happens to our Jack, it's thy fault"*. Even when I went home for the first time in uniform, my Dad told me, *"Now you want to get some medals!"*

Under training

Just two weeks later I arrived at *HMS Collingwood*, which certainly came as an eye-opener! We were first introduced to our training Chief, who took us all off to

A real sailor at last - 17 years old!

be kitted out. Next morning, our first job was to be marched off down the road to the barber's shop. Two of the barbers had been 'called up' from Saville Row, London, along with others from different salons, and they were top class hairdressers, who gave us the full treatment. *"What style would you like, sir?"* they asked - what a joke! We all got the same 'four-penny one' style, like it or lump it, combed straight down and cropped off, two inches above the eyes. Some of the lads went spare, especially those who'd sported shiny swept-back *Brylcreem* styles. *"Why have you cut it so short?"* they protested. The answer came back, sharp and clear, *"So it won't hang in your eyes if you have to swim for it!"* To really rub it in, when they gave us a mirror to see the rear view, we looked like a row of targets at a coconut shy! I was the lucky one really, as the 'Navy cut' wasn't too different to the 'Army cut' that I'd always had.

The drill certainly gave you discipline, but it also shook a few up. The gun drill was a bit hairy when that breech-block smacked over. The food wasn't exactly like you got at home either, that's for sure. A few meals you didn't like but, after a week, you either ate everything – even the doormat - or went hungry! One member of our room, 'Smudger' Smith, was a terrible snorer, he sounded like an angry buzz saw - it was a hell of a job to get to sleep. We were still sleeping in beds there, not hammocks. So one night we carried him out of barracks, still asleep in his bed, nothing could wake him when he started to snore. We put his bed out on the parade ground, where it was freezing.

During the night it started snowing, but he still slept on. Next morning we all fell in on parade, old Smudger still lying there in his bed. The Chief shook him awake, while the parade was creased up. The Commander wasn't very pleased either, but you could detect a slight grin just below the surface. It was comical to see Smudger in his bare feet while two other ratings carried the bed – and him – off parade. On another similar night, we hoisted him, still asleep, onto the rafters, which must have been about ten feet off the ground. He nearly broke his neck when he woke up! The daft things you do eh? You don't think of the danger as young lads.

Later we were issued with rifles and blanks, what a silly thing to do! One of the lads was changing his pants and, when he bent over, this idiot put a blank cartridge in his rifle, then dropped a pencil down the barrel. He then aimed at the rear end on display and the pencil went through both cheeks of his backside - I have never seen anybody jump as high in my life. After a mere six weeks of training, we had been transformed into 'real sailors', we now considered that we were already 'old sweats'. Ha-ha, what a joke, my God, if only we knew what was coming.

Stamshaw Camp

We were then sent off to Stamshaw Camp, Cosham, for drafting, all of us as green as grass. It was the first time we'd ever had to 'sling a hammock'. An old Leading Seaman (LS), who I innocently thought was a nice chap, used to buy me bars of chocolate - I was only seventeen. One of the older men put his hand over his mouth and said, *"Look son, I realise you are only a boy, but watch that dirty old sod"*. The following night, the LS 'tried his hand', if you'll pardon the expression, while I was asleep in my hammock, it came as quite a shock to me. But at that time I was a strapping thirteen stone, so I put my hand against the wall and, as the hammock swung, I belted him as hard as I could. He went straight down and out, pole-axed, and several cheers went up. But being just an Ordinary Seaman (OS), and having just clobbered a leading hand, I was scared to death. But nothing was said or done, he was guilty and on the following day he was drafted.

In the same camp, we also had some Indian matelots (sailors) and several Aussies. The Indians were frozen in our climate, poor devils. The Aussies had a white bull terrier as their mascot. We had a little fox terrier and, one day, the bull terrier had ours by the throat and was killing it. Guys were belting it with broom-handles but could not break its hold. At that moment, somebody lit a fag so I turned round quick and grabbed his matches. I took several of the matches in a bunch and struck them. Straight away I stuck the lighted bundle under his testicles – the dog's that is! He gave a terrific howl and beat the speed record up the parade ground, but I was lucky not to get bitten.

While waiting for our draft chits, we were employed on working parties in the dockyard. One job was in *'HMS Wrestler'*, it was quite a laugh. We were nearly all young and unknowing, so we got caught out several times by the old hands. My first time, I was sent down to the engine room to collect a 'long stand'. I saw the Chief Stoker and he took me just above the engine onto a little platform, where he told me to wait a while. I stood there for nearly an hour until the sweat was running down my back. Eventually, the Chief returned and looked me up and down. *"Are you still here son?"* he asked. My answer was, *"Well, you told me to stand here"*. He grinned and slowly proclaimed, *"Son, you are still learning, you have now had your long stand!"* I was also sent to pick up the key to the 'starboard watch'. That eventually turned into a tour of the ship and after that I didn't get caught again - I had grown up!

Whale Island

On my gunnery course at Whale Island, I started learning all over again. We were all stood to attention and the Chief then asked for six volunteers to play a piano. There were several Officers training there, and most were college lads. Six of them promptly jumped forward, but then came the shock! Six sheets of emery paper were issued out and they were told to clean all the cannons around the parade ground. Another lesson well learned - never get caught as a volunteer!

My next shock came while we were doing rifle drill. We had 'presented arms' from the 'shoulder arms' position about twenty-five times. Then, all of a sudden, the Chief shouted out, *"Order arms!"* OS Dunn was still presenting arms of course and there was a moment of complete silence before the order rang out, *"Dunn, come out here!"* I ran out at the double. *"Can you hold your rifle at arm's length?"* he asked. *"Yes Sir, easy"*, came my instant but naïve reply. That was a big mistake, as his next order was, *"Right then. Round the island, with your rifle at arm's length, double!"*

It was easy for ten minutes, but I had to run around the back of all the gunnery sections. Behind each section was an air-raid shelter, joy at last. Now out of sight, I had just got the butt of the rifle to the ground, when a voice rang out. *"Pick that bloody rifle up, Dunn!"* By the time I got back to the parade ground, my chest was heaving, my shirt was sticking to me and I could not get my breath. I was near to collapse. I finally 'fell in', then the evil so-and-so suddenly said, *"Right, we will now have a little running up and down the bank of the zoo!"*

I was quickly losing my 'wet behind the ears' attitude, but then a humorous thing happened. In the zoo there were several animals, including a very old lion. He had no teeth and was completely harmless, his keeper could do anything with him. The lion walked out of his cage while it was being cleaned out and, at the same time, the pretty old 'Chief Buffer' was coming up the road on his 28" pushbike. He had only one speed, dead slow. He happened to glance back and the lion was just behind him. I have never seen a bike increase speed so much in three seconds in my life! They also had their own pig farm down on Whale Island and the old 'three badge' men who were detailed to look after it had a pretty cushy number.

Waiting for 'the draft'

My relief at leaving the island was great, but I must admit that it 'makes a man out of you'. Then it was back to RNB to await a draft chit. We never had much cash, my money in those days was just over a quid (£1) per week. At night, an old matelot used to run what was called a 'fraz board'. You simply had to find the Joker. All four suits were laid out, all mixed up – Ace, Jack, King, Queen and Two. The rest of the pack was not used. One card went under the hat and you placed your money, all the cards were face down. The card was taken from under the hat and whatever came out was placed where it should be, all cards turned up were paid. All the survivors were coming in with cash, as hundreds of pounds were won and lost. One loser asked 'stripey' if he wanted to buy an overcoat, he tried it on and it fitted perfectly. It should have done, because he had just bought his own coat – but he saw the funny side of it.

I had a good job in the RNB. I was now a leading hand, with two ratings, one shovel, one broom and a wheelbarrow. Every time the council horse and cart came in to pick up gash and rubbish, we followed it. If the old nag 'dropped its load', we promptly picked it up – still steaming - and spread it around the roses outside the wardroom. The

Chief at the main gate had a standing joke, he used to buy me a doughnut to go with the manure, rotten sod! We used to get our soap coupons issued in the drill hall. After the issue, I used to go back and pick up soap and shampoo, then take them home to my mother, as it was hard for her to get soap in those days.

I then got drafted to Northern Parade School, which had been taken over by the RN. One of my duties was patrol at night in the streets of Cosham. Between the American Army lads, both black and white, an Irish Regiment, and the usual matelots, there were some right old punch-ups at night. The American Shore Police were a great bunch, I remember their Sergeant was the biggest black man I had ever seen. He used to stand outside the *White Swan* pub with his truncheon and always had a large cigar burning, while his feet were a large size fourteen. Whenever a fight started, he used to stand at the door. As the Yanks and matelots poured out, he would push the Navy lads to one side. The Yanks, he used to pick up with one hand, tap them with his stick, and say, *"Sorry, Bud"*. It was quite a laugh!

There was never any trouble with the black Yanks. We had a call one night, as there was a disturbance in the grounds of the VD Hospital – if you don't know what that is, don't ask! We arrived in a few short minutes. There were several prostitutes in an air-raid shelter, 'taking on' VD patients! You can imagine the state of the women. On one of my runs ashore, as we were always so hungry, I went and stood in the queue for a few chips. As I got to the counter, the manager said, *"Sorry sailor, only scraps left"*. Luckily, just in front of me was a young girl, who turned around and said, *"Let him have my chips"*. And that's how I met my future wife! I tried my best to find out where she lived, she tried to put me off, but I won in the end. I then got my draft chit but hadn't a clue as to where we were heading. However, there was the train, waiting alongside the barracks, so we all climbed aboard and set off north.

The Girl from the Chip Shop

On convoy out of Liverpool

We had been travelling for about three hours and were all parched, dying for a drink, but there was no water in the toilets. Then they came around with a helping of plain bread rolls - no butter or margarine - and boiled eggs. Have you ever tried eating bread rolls and boiled eggs with no drink, we couldn't even swallow! Eventually we arrived at the port of Liverpool and went straight on to a troopship. We were laid up there for three days, awaiting the convoy to assemble. We eventually set off in pitch darkness and started the 'Zig-zag' course that all convoys stuck to. I think the ship was called the *'Arbosses'*, she belonged to the *Elder Dempster* line. One thing I **do** remember is that we were packed in like the proverbial sardines! We sailed close to the Azores, to put the German submarines off, before heading for Freetown (the capital of Sierra Leone, West Africa).

It was as hot as hell in Freetown, not a breath of fresh air it seemed - no wonder they called it 'the white man's grave'. The local 'bumboats' came out to greet us and the natives used to dive out of their canoes for coins. We'd been told that they'd only dive for 'silver', so we used to cover a halfpenny with silver paper – we called this the 'Glasgow tanner' - and throw it in. They used to dive down for it, then come up shaking their fists and shouting, *"You set me up Johnny!"* One of those local natives was built like a heavyweight boxer, with a hell of a figure. We found out that he was later shot as a spy, and we heard that he used to get information of where ships were going, then pass this on to the enemy.

We carried on with our 'Zig-zag' pattern all the way down to Cape Town, on the southern tip of South Africa. Those coastal waters were alive with U-boats and we had a few scares, but we didn't lose any ships. I was standing outside the ship's Regulation Office when they piped for a volunteer to join a minesweeper in the Simon's Town naval base. Now, we'd recently heard that we might have had to serve as a naval detachment in the desert. Not fancying being the rear-gunner on a camel, I jumped into the office, even before the operator had switched off, to volunteer my services. And so I joined *'HMS Shapinsay'*, as one of her crew happened to be off sick. That lasted a month, until he came back, so I was then posted to Klaver Camp, which was a naval magazine above Simon's Town, its purpose to supply ships with ammunition. This was a real education, as the place was situated in a deep mountain valley.

The Great Dane

In the naval base, the men kept a huge Great Dane as their mascot. They treated him as a sailor, by the name of 'Able Seaman (AB) Just Nuisance'. He even used to go ashore with the lads, joining them on the train, with twenty-three stations to Cape Town in a journey of twenty-five miles. Nuisance hated coloureds, so the local people were very frightened of him. My first encounter with him was in the 'United Services Institute' (USI). I went in for a bed and there was only the one left. I couldn't make out why there were sly grins all round. Then, at midnight, I found out! I was happily lying in bed one minute, the next I was flat on the floor. Nuisance had a bed like any sailor - I

Making Friends!

didn't argue, he was a very big dog. I think he eventually died of poisoning from a rusty food tin. There is still a memorial to him in Simon's Town, and there was a book about him too. If he was ever late coming back into the base, he was confined to barracks, what a dog!

(The above story of 'AB Just Nuisance RN' was later confirmed to me by Jack's grandson, David, who sent me details of a web-site, which contained a full account of the story. The dog began its life in 1937 and its owner later moved to Simon's Town to run the USI. He was a very friendly dog and was regularly treated to tit-bits by the many sailors who passed through the naval base. He started following them on board their ships, with HMS Neptune becoming his firm favourite. Here, he would lie on deck at the top of the gangway and generally get in the way, due to his size. When the sailors started calling him 'a nuisance', the name stuck.

Jack's memory of the dog riding on the train is borne out by the web-site story, but the Railway Company eventually couldn't put up with that any longer and threatened to have him put down. Many and loud were the protests, to such an extent that letters were written to the Commander-in-Chief RN. The outcome was that it was decided to enrol the dog as an official rating into the RN! That happened on August 25th 1939, but that was one sailor who never went to sea!

AB Nuisance did much to raise the morale of the sailors at Simon's Town, but was eventually discharged on New Year's Day 1944, after having been diagnosed with a thrombosis after a motor accident. It was decided to 'put him to sleep' and he was laid to rest in the Naval Hospital on April 2nd. Jack's memory of a 'rusty food tin' appears to be just a rumour! There is still a statue of Just Nuisance in Jubilee Square and his grave is still a regular stopping point for visitors to Red Hill. Also, the Simon's Town Museum contains a wealth of documentation and photographs in memory of this remarkable dog. Ed.)

Klaver Camp

Standing guard at night was a thriller, as there were baboons everywhere, accompanied by a lot of snakes and scorpions. My guard companion was a guy called Charlie Pierce. He was so nervous at being on guard at night that I swear he could go to sleep while still standing up. One night he was standing alongside the barbed-wire fence, no doubt fast asleep, when a huge baboon came up alongside him and started sniffing. I could see from my position that Charlie hadn't seen the animal, so I gave a blast on my signal whistle, with which we were all supplied. Charlie woke up with a start and then spotted the baboon. He dropped his rifle and went past me at three-minute mile pace, right back to the base, about a mile distant. He never went on guard again.

We used to 'sling our hammocks' in a tin shed that was laughingly called the Guardroom. We used to do stints of four hours on and four hours off. I was sleeping in my hammock one night, about twelve o'clock, when I felt a tickle on my chest. Being pretty hairy myself, I slowly opened my eyes and there was the hairiest bloody spider I have ever seen, creeping up my chest. I've never left a hammock so quickly in my life! I never even knew if it was dangerous or not, I just gave it the benefit of my doubt. Scorpions were another hazard, you had to check your shoes each time before you put them on. You also learned not to throw stones at the baboons, as they were very good shots with their return stones. In the breeding season, they often entered the little enclave of Simon's Town, raiding the shops and scaring people half to death.

One afternoon, I was patrolling around the magazine and, as I came around this big boulder, there was this very large snake, reared up and hissing. Now if there's one thing I hate it is snakes, so I quickly ran back to the Guardroom to get Sammy. He was a young Zulu worker who used to clean for us and make the tea. I told him about the snake, so he grabbed a sack and followed me to the boulder. Discretion being the better part of valour, I let him go first of course and, when we saw the snake, he started to bait it. It

In Cape Town ready for a 'Run Ashore'

kept striking at him but, after a few minutes, it wavered one way. Sammy went in like a flash, grabbed it behind the head and the snake was in the sack.

Two weeks later, he came in with two snakeskin ties, made from the snake - they were great. A few days after that, I happened to catch him out at an illegal practice! He had made two small bowls of clay, joined together with a straw, and a long reed to suck through. It was what was known as a 'bubbly pipe'. There was water in one bowl and a herb called 'daker', picked from the mountainside, in the other. Sammy told me that the Zulus used to take it when they went to war, believing that, even if they were hit with a bullet, they would still run for a hundred yards before they dropped. But now, if caught using it, it was a prison sentence straight away. He went down on his knees and begged me not to drop him in it. He was only young and a great worker so I gave in and, after that, he would do anything for me. After working for six months, the young Zulu workers would go back to their kraals and lay back with their wives for the next six months. Then, when the money had gone, they would come back south and work again.

One member of our mess was a 'Scouser', a native of Liverpool, and he was the biggest rogue I've ever met. *(As a Scouser myself, I won't take exception with Jack on this – I've met quite a few myself! Ed.)* He was an addict for tattoos, his whole body was absolutely covered in pictures of all sorts. He had the famous 'fox and hounds' scene all down his back, so you can guess just where the fox's brush disappeared! He could never remember when he had the tattoos done, because he was always drunk at the time. It's a good job he was only allowed ashore only once a month. He had somehow got hold of some daker and he used to smoke it before he went ashore. There, he often used to get into fights and he never felt anything until next day, when he woke up in the cells.

I had two months at Klaver Camp, before I was again drafted, this time to *'HMS Southern Pride'*.

On board the whaler

She was an ex-whaling ship, not the fleet 'mother ship', but one of the smaller ships that used to do the actual whale catching. At the outbreak of war, her Norwegian crew had brought her across from their homeland to England. The harpoon gun had been removed from the bows and replaced with a 4" gun, on which I was the gun-layer. The rest of our armament consisted of a *Lewis* gun aft, two *Hotchkiss* on the bridge and about one hundred and fifty depth charges – she was literally a floating bomb!

My stand-by watch was at a steam gun behind the funnel and I had never seen anything like it. It was like a trench mortar, you simply dropped hand grenades down the barrel. It had a twist grip, just like a motorbike, which was connected to a steam-pipe from the engine room. I asked the skipper what it was for and I nearly died laughing. His answer was, *"It's for bringing down low-flying aircraft"*. Not a hope – there was no gun shield, so it was a certain one-way ticket to the life hereafter! Later in my tour,

I scrounged a load of old spuds from the galley and used the weapon to play havoc with the chasing seagulls! Good job the skipper never caught me.

We were based in Cape Town and, when a convoy approached, it was our job to patrol the waters around the Cape of Good Hope and across Table Bay. I have never seen waves so large in my life. I used to do a watch 'at the wheel' and also at a lookout position on the stern. Because I was the youngest OS, I was always muggins for the stern lookout. Also, I was the only rating who was not part of the normal patrol service. The stern position was a platform, six-foot high and only two-foot square, situated between two rows of depth charges. If ever we got hit, I would be the first in line, knocking at the 'Pearly Gates'.

The platform had a belt, which I had to clip onto the rail to stop falling into the sea. At times, when the weather was really rough, the waves could be twenty to thirty feet high. I was sometimes six feet under water for about a minute. When it got really bad, I would ring the bridge and ask to stand behind the smokestack. The skipper's answer was always, *"Maintain your position, Dunn"*. I think it was probably around that time that I decided that I wanted to be a diver, as I was spending more time under the water than on top anyway! *(My description of the skipper at the same time would have put him as 'a child of doubtful parentage'.)*

In that dreadful weather, the mess deck always used to be two or three inches deep in water. The crew all had bunks of course, but I had to sling my hammock under a hatch, where it often used to get flooded. It got to the point when I began to sleep on the mess deck itself, with my foot wrapped around the leg of a table to stop me falling off. It was really rough. We had that job for six months and we used to get 'hard lines' money for it, which worked out as just a few coppers a day extra. Apparently, the well-known Lady Astor tried to stop it. She'd been out on a destroyer on a really calm day and stated that there was no need for extra pay. So she then pretty quickly joined the skipper on my list as mentioned above!

We used to get *'HMS Queen Mary'* and *'HMS Queen Elizabeth'* (we called her *'Lizzie'*) coming into Cape Town, loaded then with prisoners of war (POWs). When we used to head out on patrol, we used to go alongside those magnificent liners on our way out. In those seas, one minute we were forty feet below their guard rail, then next minute we could have shaken hands with the people on their decks. I suppose, by comparison, we must have looked like a little duck bobbing about, but those mighty Queens never even moved.

One day on patrol, we had the sea crashing in on our starboard side. The 2nd Lieutenant was trying to get from the stern to forward, when a wave caught him and washed him over the side. I was making a run for it from the stern, when another wave washed him back aboard and I managed to grab him. He never forgot it and nor did I. Whenever there was no convoy duty, the crew used to go into Simon's Town and get a bit of shore leave. One day, there was just a couple of us left on board, myself as acting duty quartermaster and a Sub-lieutenant in charge. He then informed me that the dockyard Captain was soon expected. I had the wind up, as I did not have a Bosun's pipe. But I'd always been able to 'take off' (imitate) the pipe, so I took a chance. The Captain duly arrived and I 'piped him aboard' with no pipe. I got away with it, he never cottoned on, Ha-ha.

For the rest of the day, I spent the time fishing with a hand-line. There were literally hundreds of mackerel. I had a tin bath alongside me to put them in, so Taffy the Cook had them nice and fresh. I was still hanging over the side, pulling them in, when I caught a 'real big one'. Just as I was hauling it in, I was about a foot from the water, a big head came out of the water, covered in bristles and with big shiny eyes. It took the fish and left me with just the head. It was only a seal, but I was so surprised that I fell back on the deck, frightened to death! Another good catch, which took no effort at all, was the flying fish. We had a low gunwale, so they used to fly on board every day off the African coast. We'd just cut their wings off and they were great to eat

We left Cape Town for the coast of West Africa, to escort a cable ship called *'Lady Dennis Pender'*, manned mostly by a St Helena crew. They were laying underwater cable off the African coast. We called into St Helena - what a place that was, no wonder Napoleon never got away. We were able to anchor in only one spot, as the water was very deep. There was only one vehicle on the island, which belonged to a small Army detachment. I don't know why the Army was there, as it is 1,000 miles from the African coast. They had a ship only about every two months, everything had to be brought in by sea. The coloured inhabitants were very nice, though it was difficult to understand what they said. Some had a French accent, being descendants of Napoleon's staff, some had British accents from the British guards, while the remainder had the African voices of their slave forefathers. But at least everybody spoke English. The island was very poor, seeing a ship about once a month. Their main crop was sisal, which was used for making rope. The locals also made lace, with belts and bracelets made from seeds and berries from the bushes. The girls were very good looking, oh dear me!

We then headed for Jakaradi, on the Gold Coast. On the way there, we picked up an empty lifeboat – there were no survivors and no oars, but all the provisions and water supplies were intact. There were several heaps of clothes, as if the people had stepped out of them. There was no identification of any kind, either on the clothes or marked on the boat, so we towed it in to port. To this day, we never did learn the story. A bit like that famous *Marie Celeste* mystery I suppose. We had to anchor both fore and aft, as there was no jetty to tie-up to. We all went over the side for a swim but, within five minutes a port official came racing along the shore yelling at us that swimming was forbidden.

We went ashore and got a taxicab to Seccondi. The cabs were open-back *Ford Pilots*, with planks laid across for seating. You had to hang on to the planks, put your trust in the Lord and keep your bowels open! I think that those taxis must be one of the wonders of the world. We went through native villages flat out - goats, pigs, chickens and turkeys, we just went hell for leather, straight through them all. It was so hair-raising, that we decided to walk the four miles back.

On arrival, we walked around one corner and there was this black dentist, with his patients all sat on a log. There was no such thing as anaesthetic, he just pulled the teeth straight out. He caught me watching and invited me as the next patient - no deal! On our walk back, a local girl tried to sell us two guinea fowl, which were still alive. We refrained, but she followed us back the whole four miles. I felt rather sorry for her, she wanted two and six each for the birds. We explained that we could not kill and pluck them. Straight away she sat on the side of the jetty, wrung their necks and plucked them, the dock was covered in feathers.

They catered for Sunday dinner on the seaman's mess-deck and we soon became sick of yams. Taffy the Cook tried to roast them, but they came out like concrete. We had no bread for two months, just hardtack biscuits, but they constipated you. When you went to the toilet, you needed an oilcan and a screwdriver!

Green bananas

Our next port of call was back to Freetown where, as we landed, a black lady was roasting peanuts, which we just had to taste. She had two little boys, about nine or ten. She asked, *"Do you want to buy a chicken?"* The chickens were all running about and we had to pick the one we wanted. I pointed to the one I wanted, but they looked like game fowl to me. One of the lads caught the chicken, picked up a palm leaf, which he put over the chicken's head - and then screwed its head off. The lady said it would be ready-cooked by the time we had been for a swim. When we got to Lumley Beach, several black girls came along and sold us some bananas. I bought a complete stem of them, they were so green that I reckoned they would keep until we got home. Our next stop was to collect the chicken. It was presented on a palm leaf, with a piece of native bread. The cost was only two-and-six and it was just delicious.

We next called in at Casablanca, on the north-western coast of Africa in Morocco, this was just after the Americans had invaded and several French ships had been sunk. As we walked into town, an American was sat on a bit of grass, with his gun held across his knees and a bottle of beer in the other hand. He greeted us with *"Hiya Limeys"*. I asked him what he was doing, as he wasn't stood to attention. He grinned and pointed to several mounds behind him. *"I'm guarding my buddies that were killed during the invasion"*. I said, *"Why guard them?"* and he answered, *"The doggone Arabs keep digging them up and stealing their gear"*.

We carried on into town, where we had a drink with some members of the French Foreign Legion. Amazingly, they could all speak good English. A taxi pulled up outside and I couldn't believe it. It was a nice taxi all right, but I was astonished to see a pair of shafts on the front, and a camel was pulling it, as there was no petrol available. We had no food left on board, but all the Americans could supply was eggs and cornflakes. By the time we got to Gibraltar, we were all egg-bound!

Then, on the way up to Gibraltar, I went down with dysentery, no doubt due to the green bananas! I lost three stone and literally lived on the toilet. The trouble was, there was only the one toilet between thirty men, so if anybody else wanted to use it, they would lift me off and put me on the guardrail. Then, business done, they would put me back on the throne. At 'The Rock', they put me in a rest camp for a week, as I was in a pretty bad way. That week did me the world of good, while my behind returned back to its original condition. And, at last, we were on the way back home.

We arrived in North Shields in February for a boiler clean. Both watches got leave and I was due to leave the ship for Whale Island. But, before I left North Shields, one of the dockers told me his little girl had lost a leg in the air raids and had never seen a banana. So 'big softie' came up with six bananas. During the following week, there was about thirty dockers turned up, each father to a one-legged girl, and I was eventually left with just six bananas. They say that there is one born every minute! I left the ship and headed south. (I found out fifty years later, that the *'Southern Pride'* went down with a Russian Convoy, a week after I left. There were no survivors.)

Ducking and diving!

It was nice having a bit of leave, after which I reported to Whale Island Bay, what an education! As soon as you went over the footbridge, you had to run everywhere, and that included the officers. It certainly taught discipline. I started my first ever course on diving, lectures to start with and then into the diving boat. For the very first time I was rigged up in the suit - twenty-pound boots, twenty-pound weights and then your helmet screwed tightly on. Then it was 'climb on the ladder', and lean back to get your front glass on.

The entrance to Whale Island

I quickly lost all touch with the outside world. The water lapped up the front glass and then I grabbed the short rope and dropped down to the mud on the bottom of Pompey Harbour. I landed like a sack of coal and then had to adjust the air control, which partly inflated the suit. I could then just about walk around, as the black sticky mud was very deep. If one struggles too much, or panics, one can get CO2 (carbon dioxide) poisoning, which renders you unconscious. It's amazing how much rubbish there is down there; oil drums, cables, ropes, and gash from the ships.

My first job as a diver was on a minesweeper. The skipper used to take his teeth out to eat his breakfast and, when he was finished, the steward would take the cloth, with bits of bread and crumbs, and shake it over the side. Unfortunately, on one occasion, along with the crumbs went the skipper's teeth. The job was reported as a 'fouled screw' and the skipper said there would be 'a packet of fags' in it if I found his teeth. Trouble was, I didn't smoke! But I dropped over the side anyway and soon hit the bottom. I found one set straight away and just put them in the top of my boots.

As we used to get five shillings an hour extra for diving, I decided to sit on a sunken oil drum for half-an-hour to make a few bob! Then I dug about in the mud again - potato peelings, bits of bacon, a few eels and loads of rusty tin cans - before I went up to the surface with the one set of teeth. Skip was overjoyed and he then promised me a bottle of rum if I found the other set. He was dead keen to have that second set, as there were a lot of gold teeth amongst them. I went down again and, after scraping around for a while, eventually found the second set. Skip nearly kissed me when I surfaced – and I finished up with 400 fags and a pint of rum.

Two weeks later, we had a call to Esher Pontoon. They had lots of small craft alongside to provision, so it was inevitable that some goods would fall out of the nets and a gallon of rum had duly gone over the side. Under our diving boat, we had two or three cup-hooks screwed into the keel so that, if we found anything, we would tie a bit of cod-line around it and hang our loot underneath the boat. We found that particular rum - and another one – so they both went 'on the hook'. We then went out into Portchester Creek and had a 'bit of a do'!

Having qualified as a diver, I was then ready for a draft and the fateful day duly arrived. *"Report with kit and hammock to railway sidings in the barracks."* We set off that night, about 1,000 of us, and I was drafted to the *'Iron Duke'* as a diver. The *'Iron Duke'* had been run ashore when she was hit and then used as a drafting ship. The funniest job I ever had was when I was piped to rig the diving boat. When I reported to the quarterdeck, the diving officer told me to draw a shovel and then took me to the starboard waist, near the galley. The story was that, every time we were issued with tins of herrings we promptly walked to the starboard side and dumped them - herrings for breakfast didn't go down very well. The trouble was, when the tide went out, a golden pyramid could be seen just below the surface! The Admiral at Scapa would have taken off if he'd seen it on his visit. So I had to go down and level off the pyramid.

The spot was alive with crabs, so the Chief Cook said, *"Get a good one and I will cook it and we'll have half each"*. I told him I'd have a go. Down I went and, on top of an old battery, was the biggest crab I have ever seen. I went down on my knees in front of it and it reared up, with its claws at the ready. Like an idiot, I waved my hand in front of it and slowly brought my other hand up behind it, not realising that its eyes could see backwards as well, its eyes being on the end of those antennae. It suddenly whipped around and caught my thumb - it was bloody agony, just like a pair of pliers and it didn't let go until I got back in the boat. The Chief Cook was over the moon – *"Can you get me another one tomorrow?"* My answer was, *"Get your head in the sea securing position and get stuffed!"*

Another little job we had was for the local fisherman from Long Hope, they used to set their lobster pots about ten yards from the ship. The Chief Cook gave me a bottle of rum and what I had to do was take a lobster from a pot, then put the lobster pot back with the rum inside. We then went on board, onto the bridge, and watched with binoculars as the fisherman came to empty his pots. He pulled up his pot and you could see him laughing his head off and having a swig from the bottle. It was a good exchange.

A week later I was on watch as quartermaster, when we received a message from the shore base that some prisoners from a U-boat were coming aboard. There were about twenty-two of them, tied together and blindfolded, so they couldn't see the fleet anchorage. Two were brought aboard dead and I was told to order two coffins from Stromness. I said, *"Why should they get coffins, when we only get a hammock and a fire bar?"* I nearly got put in the rattle! As the submariners came on board they dropped their escape kit at the top of the gangway. It was beautiful gear, so one was 'lifted' into my diving store - it would be ideal for diving in the summer. I had it for just one hour, they missed it, and guessed who had knocked it off, so hard luck!

Service on an aircraft carrier

The draft chit arrived, sending me to the aircraft carrier *'HMS Formidable'*. We arrived on board, all 2,300 of us, it was the first big ship I had been sent to. We started trials and gunnery shoots for about two weeks and then the buzz went around the ship that we were heading north. We had no clue where we were going. There were lots of flying off and deck landings, with quite a few 'prangs'. It was very hairy, sitting in the director as the planes came in, especially if they missed the arrester wire! I was on one lookout watch on the bridge; it was very frosty, as we weren't very far from Arctic waters. A stanchion on the bridge was all colours of the rainbow, heavy with frost and, like an idiot, I put my tongue out to touch it. My tongue stuck to it, ye Gods! Luckily, at just that moment the 'purser's key' had just arrived and I poured it straight down the stanchion, thank God my tongue was released.

We then received the news that we were going to 'have a go' at the German battleship *'Tirpitz'*, she was holed up in one of those narrow fjords (inlets) in Norway. The aim was to keep her confined in the fjord, to stop her coming out and attacking shipping in the North Sea. The brass knew they couldn't sink her with Carrier-based aircraft, but could at least damage her. The only trouble was, as soon as the Germans got a hint of an attack, they started their smoke machines up on both sides of the fjord. These would fill the fjord with a smokescreen, thus covering the whole ship, so that the attacking aircraft could not focus. Our only hope was to surprise them. The torpedo bombers, being slower, could not get a hit, so they rigged the *'Seafires'* (naval version of the *'Spitfire'*) to carry 800-pound bombs.

The Squadron Leader's brother ran the *Tannoy* system on board and used to relay the attacks all round the ship. One of these attacks was in progress, when his brother's aircraft was hit. The brother radioed back to the ship that he has been hit and couldn't get out of his aircraft. Instead, he aimed his craft towards the screws of the *'Tirpitz'*. He lost his life and must have been the first British 'Kamikaze' pilot. We landed several hits on the Nazi ship, but our bombs could not sink her. The RAF was then called in, with 10,000-pound bombs, which finally overturned her. The Germans managed to get several survivors out, through cutting a hole in her hull while she was upside down. We finished that operation and returned to old Scapa Flow.

We all expected a few days leave at least, but got a nasty surprise instead - they were going to send us straight out to the Pacific, without any leave at all. Capt Keene was the Skipper, his last ship had been the *'Maidstone'*. He cleared lower decks to talk to the ship's company, announcing that we were going straight out to the Far East. It was the closest I have ever been to a mutiny, catcalls rang across the flight deck. He was furious and said he would not hesitate to order his Royal Marines to fire aft at the crew. The ship was in turmoil but, after a couple of days, a message came from the Admiralty to give both watches a week's leave - great relief.

Home for a spell

The trip back down to Hampshire took thirty-six hours, with the ferry-trip across to Thurso particularly terrible. We suffered very rough seas, it was like the Bay of Biscay. Many were forced 'down below', all different forces, and I wondered what the big dustbins were for. I had stopped on the upper deck but it started to rain, as well as freezing, so I went below. I then found out what the bins were for! It was chaos below - everybody was being sick, they were all round the bins, while those who couldn't reach were aiming from a distance. Thus the bodies draped around the bins were themselves smothered in vomit. I quickly returned to the upper deck!

At that moment, they piped that the canteen was open and I was first in line to get a cup of tea. I then looked for something to eat but whoever ran the canteen must have been an agent of the devil. There was no sugar to start with and the only food was herring sandwiches – with no marge, just dry bread. Can you imagine what the men were feeling like when they had been throwing up for an hour, only to be met with herring sandwiches? I never saw one sandwich bought!

On leaving Scapa, I had brought ten dozen eggs. There were plenty of eggs in Scapa, besides sheep – but that's another story! We boarded the train at Thurso, then had to stand all the way to Edinburgh, before continuing all the way, still without a seat, down to London's Euston Station. I stood as long as possible, but slowly finished up on the floor, still guarding my eggs. Alongside me on the floor was an ATS girl. By the time we got into London, I'd had no drink, was covered in fag ends and badly needed a shave – but at least the eggs were still intact!

We got across to Waterloo, good old Southern Railway, and another two hours to get home. You may not believe it, still no bloody seats, the train was choc-a-bloc with forces personnel. I was so tired that I just had to have a kip, so I climbed up into the luggage rack. But at fourteen stone, the rack gave in and I then found out I hadn't got a mother or father. Well at least that's what they told me - they didn't like fourteen stone landing on them from a great height! The leave flashed by all too soon I'm afraid. My girlfriend Bren lived down in Cosham, but she came up to my home. On the last day, my Mum asked what would I like to eat before I went back. Now I was very fond of onions, so I told her I wanted a plate of fried onions, about a pound-and-a-half. It was lovely!

An unscheduled stop-over

Back on board, everybody was well and truly 'cheesed off' now that the leave was over. We then participated in sea trials and some gunnery, before sailing off to the Far East. We arrived in Gibraltar – or 'Gib' as it was called - and immediately broke down, our main bearing had given up. The local dockyard said they couldn't fix it, but our Engineering Officer was brilliant. He asked if he could borrow one of the large cranes. Then he ordered the bearing from North Shields, to be brought out by a fast destroyer. He then cut out each deck, lifted them out and laid them on the flight deck until he got to the main bearing. He then fitted the new bearing, which weighed about six tons, replaced each deck and then re-welded everything back into place. It was a fantastic operation, seeing as the dockyard could not do it.

But that job took about seven months to do and, while we were based there in Gib, the skipper made us run around and over The Rock, it nearly killed us. While we were in dry dock, lots of us caught a nasty stomach bug called 'Rock Tummy'. It was awful, as our heads (toilets) couldn't be used on board, with being in dry dock. Instead we had to use the dockside toilets. You'd get halfway down the gangway, a very slippery incline, and then the bug would hit you, no warning. Not much fun, I can tell you!

PT & sports on deck

We had PT sessions on the flight deck, and the PTI came up to me and said, *"You are boxing tonight"*. I told him to 'get lost' but he told me it wasn't a request - but an order.

In my mess was Johnny King, ex-champion flyweight, he used to get me to spar with him. So at least I had a good idea of what to do. We were detailed to be fighting a team from the Army ashore and all my messmates turned up. I had been picked out because of my weight and my fifty-inch chest, so I was first in the ring - I was scared to death to be honest.

When the 'Pongo' (Navy term for a soldier) climbed into the ring, I nearly died. He had a cauliflower ear, was cross-eyed, and with a flat nose. He came out arms akimbo, looking like a punch block, I thought he was going to kill me. But he had no guard so, in desperation, I stepped in 'southpaw style', being left-handed and hit him with everything I had. It was a bit of luck, but I must have hit him hard, because the next thing I knew, he was on his back and counted out first round. Two days later, he asked me for a return fight - thank God the ship was sailing in two days time!

After the fight, the other two divers asked me ashore for a drink, to celebrate my win. I didn't drink, but I still went. We went into what we called a 'boiled oil' shop, which was just a nickname of course. I was asked if I liked gin, which of course I'd never tried. So up came a full bottle of gin, six shillings worth - we got rid of that in about twenty minutes. The next diver went up for another bottle and they asked me what I thought of it, but I couldn't make out the taste of it. So we got rid of that one pretty quickly too and then it was my turn. I went up to the bar but, when I got back to the table, they were both out like a light! It hadn't affected me, so I had to get them back to the ship. I had one on my back and the other one under my arm. The Officer-of-the-watch laughed his head off, as he knew I was teetotal. I got them both into their hammocks but the next day I was 'in the doghouse'. They just couldn't believe that I had not drunk before and didn't speak to me for about two weeks.

Sailing to the Far East

We left Gibraltar for the Far East, first sailing through 'the Med' (Mediterranean Sea) to Alexandria in Egypt. A pilot who had been shore-based asked if he could have a deck-flight. So off we went to sea again for more trials and the pilot was given a kite. We turned into the wind for take-off, got up to thirty knots and the plane took off. On leaving the flight deck, all of a sudden the wings folded, both pilot and plane ended 'in the drink' and the ship went straight over both of them. There was no trace of them and I thought *"What a waste of life, he need not have flown"*. We then headed down the Suez Canal, where Italian POWs were camped along the banks in their thousands. We had a few nasty signs thrown at us and a lot of Anglo-Saxon language was exchanged. *(Everyone knows that the shortest book in the world is accepted to be the one dedicated to Italian War heroes!)*

Although supposed to do only three knots through the Canal, we bumped that up a bit, so there was a large bow-wave following us. Some way ahead was a flat-bottomed water boat, full of water jars. The Arab in charge jumped out of his boat, as he saw the large wave coming towards him. The wave hit the boat and the whole lot turned over. There was an Arab policeman on a camel and, along with the boatman, they chased us for about two miles trying to stop us - they didn't get much back! To our left was the Sinai desert, just a load of telegraph poles and sand. About a half-mile from the Canal a very large water pipe, weighing about a ton, had fallen from a lorry. We were anchored in the Bitter Lakes and several soldiers came aboard and told us that the water pipe would vanish during the night - no lorries, simply taken away by hand. When I got up at daylight to check, sure enough the pipe had gone.

Another incident took place while we were anchored. In order to keep cool, several members of the crew laid their hammocks on the deck. During the night, naked natives, covered in grease, came up the anchor cables. They tickled the men so that they rolled over, then got them to roll the other way and away went the hammock, mattress and blanket! Even if you woke up, you couldn't hold them, owing to the grease - they would pinch anything.

A land 'down under'

We continued on our way, now heading for what was to be our base in Australia. We met some terrible weather in the Australian Bight and one destroyer escort lost two ratings overboard. Permission was asked to carry out a search, but this was refused, we all had to keep position. But before we had that episode, we had called into Fremantle, just south of Perth, where they gave us a great time. Everybody on board received a 'comfort bag', they were great people in West Australia. We later arrived on the other side of the continent, in Sydney Harbour and saw the famous 'coat hanger' bridge. We 'came alongside' in a place I think was called Woolamaloo. Australia was certainly a hell of a place, with heaps of good food, as there was no rationing, and loads of girls, as nearly all the young men were away fighting in the islands.

After just a week 'down under', we set off for the Philippines islands, where Manus was the first American base we called at. Just about every time we pulled an anchor up, a waterlogged body would come up with it. We then carried on towards Japan, but on the way we first had to 'oil' a destroyer, which was something different to watch. Oiling a ship was just about the worst job you could be tasked with on board ship, but it still had to be done. The oil pipe was first hoisted out by our starboard crane. They had just connected up to the destroyer, and her stokers and about half of the ship's company were now formed up around the funnel and the boat-deck. The officers, POs and some of the crew were in whites. They signalled to us to start pumping, when - instant calamity! The pipe connection on the destroyer burst with the pressure and, within seconds, crude oil covered the crew and went all up the funnel and bridge. Around a third of the ship was quickly turned jet black and the crew looked like the *Black and White Minstrel Show* - I dread to think how long it took to clean the ship afterwards.

At one point we passed over what was the deepest spot in the ocean, I believe it was called the 'Emden Deep'. We were practising our gunnery and bumped up our record on the 4-inch turret to twenty rounds per minute. We met up with the Yanks and they trailed their drogues for even more gunnery. The whole of the American Fleet seemed to be shooting that day, I'd never seen so much flak in my life. But they never touched a target! Then we had a go – and immediately shot down the first target. So the Yanks streamed another drogue, with the same effect – not a single hit, while we hit it with our *Bofors*. After this procedure had been repeated for a third time, the Skipper sent a sarcastic signal across to the Americans – *"Have you any more targets?"* No answer was received, which wasn't too surprising!

Action in the Pacific

Our planes started 'flying off', ready for our first attack on Japan. Several targets were attacked, including Honshu, Ishe Kaki and Jami Jaki aerodromes. We were doing four-hour watches but stayed 'closed up' at the guns from dawn to dusk. It was murder, being closed up all day, then a middle watch followed by two short hours of sleep, then closed up again. After a week like that, we were staggering about like zombies. The Gunnery Officer, Lt Commander Duff, could see we were not getting much sleep, so he said that, as long as we were closed up, we could nod off on the guns. But we had a right evil so-and-so, a Petty Officer (PO), in charge of our 4-inch turret. He ignored the kind gesture from our Gunnery Officer and kept coming around the turret, poking us with a stick to keep us awake. If I could have got him against the guardrail, he would have gone over the side, honest. PO Ferret he was called – very true to his name, he even looked like one of those animals! In fact we all reckoned he was worse than the bloody Japs.

We then got a message over the *Tannoy* system, which is how we used to get news of all that was going on in the Fleet. This message was that two hundred 'bogies' were coming in from the north-east. 'Bogies' was the nickname for Japanese kites. Their spotter planes were first on the scene and none of us really knew what to expect. You do some silly things when you think you may soon be swimming for it – I had my bankbook, photographs and watch wrapped in a condom, which was knotted and hanging round my neck! I thought to myself, *"This is it mate, we are going to get plastered"*. That's the time you think of home and your whole life flashes before your eyes. Then they were on us, diving down in all directions. That is when we found out about 'the Divine Wind', or 'Kamikaze', the name given for the Japanese suicide jockeys. They certainly gave us more than just 'wind'! These *'Zero'* dive-bombers carried a 500-pound bomb and a full fuel tank. The intention was that they would crash straight through the ship's superstructure, then explode and catch fire, with all the horrific consequences. Their own lives must have meant little to them as long as they took many of ours.

As the gun-layer, I could see the little sods coming in, almost as though they were aiming directly at me. I knew our shells were hitting this particular plane, but they certainly weren't going off. So later, after the attack was over, I had to report to my Gunnery Officer and he asked, *"What went wrong?"* I told him that the lad who was setting the fuses was only a youngster and I didn't think he was setting the fuses right. There was an old timer in my mess, sixty if he was a day, but he had set the clock back a few years and managed to join up. I asked him if he would be my fuse setter, saying it wasn't fair that such a young lad should be in a turret. The old timer was chuffed to bits

Aftermath of a dive-bomber attack on HMS Formidable

and the very next day we had our first success.

We heard that the *'Indomitable'* had copped it and then it was our turn, as we took a hit at my trainer. I was the gun-layer and, as the *Zeroes* dived in, I started training the gun very slowly to get a good target. Just then, something buzzed past me and went around the inside of the turret, it sounded just like a demented bumblebee. I then started cursing at Jock McArdle, 'inviting' him to get his gun around quicker. Finally, when the attack had finished, I went to tell Jock just what I thought of him. As he turned around to answer me, I quickly lost my breakfast - his arm had gone from just below the elbow, it was hung down like a shin of beef and I was as sick as a dog. Jock had somehow kept the gun trained with only one hand, which had required some Herculean effort on a power mounting. The whole ship had been shaken and the flight deck was one hell of a mess - fire in the hanger, owing to the hole blown in the flight deck, and many aircraft also ablaze.

In the attack, I'd lost one of my messmates, an OS by the name of Charge, who was only sixteen years old. The funny thing is that I couldn't even picture what he looked like for the next six months, I suppose it was some sort of self-preserving mechanism. Charge had been on the signal-bridge when the dive-bomber hit us, he looked over the edge and the explosion took his head off. My turret crew was then ordered to leave the gun and 'fall in below' in the hanger. Our job now concerned a long line of our own bombs, stood like sentries down the centre line of the hanger. They were lined up in a long row, ready to be strapped onto their aircraft. But, because of the heat and flames, they were now getting red hot, and the aircraft could not be moved until the bombs were shifted onto the lift, to be then taken to the flight deck. It was a bit hairy, as flames from the fuel vapour kept licking towards us like snakes. It was the nearest I had been to heaven!

After the action, we were supplied with a 'corned dog' sandwich and a nice drop of tea. The scene on the flight deck was still one of utter chaos, it was red hot and steaming with the water being used to fight the fire. There was a large hole in the steel deck and we all thought, with a certain amount of hope, *"This is it, we will have to go back to Sydney. Hard luck!"* But the hole was soon filled with a combination of rubbish, aircraft chocks and quick-drying cement. Amazingly, just three short hours later, our kites were flying off on another attack. As the aircraft landed back, the turret crew would 'stand down' and literally push them onto the lift, to be quickly refuelled and stocked up once again with bombs and ammo.

The Kiwi pilot

A young 'Kiwi' (New Zealander) fighter pilot, only a little bloke, became a great favourite with the lads. After one flight, I asked of him, *"Good trip?"* and he replied, *"Great, not a scratch"*. Looking at his kite, there were holes everywhere and the tail assembly was flapping in the wind! His canopy was busted and a piece of wood was sticking in his headrest. We pulled it out, it was about eighteen inches long and there was part of a Japanese name on it. He had it polished up and later hung it in his cabin. What had happened was that he had been following his Squadron Leader in an attack on a munition ship. This ship just blew up as he got above it; he caught the full blast, which shot his kite about five hundred feet up into the air.

When he got back, he was supposed to be 'grounded' – if you can call a carrier 'ground'! When he found that his plane had been refuelled, all of a sudden he was seen running down the flight deck - he wasn't going to be left behind! I never thought he would ever come again back and he would be in a hell of a lot of trouble anyway, after disobeying orders. However, he did get back, still in one piece but only just, while his plane was now a write-off. There was a ramp on the port side and his kite was literally pushed over the side, while he ended up in 'the rattle'. Better that, we thought, than some of the tales we'd heard. Crews that had to bale out were sometimes picked up by the Japs, who instantly beheaded them and threw them back in the briny. They say you must 'forgive and forget' – but not for things like that.

When he had first joined the ship, that Kiwi wasn't allowed to fly. We learned that he had previously taken his *'Seafire'* up to a railway station and flown under the footbridge - thank God there was no train coming! That guy was close to being certified, but what a pilot. I later heard that he went through the whole war unscathed and eventually got back to NZ - a bloody miracle if you ask me. Still on the same subject, he was once involved in a raid on an airfield where they suspected the Kamikazes were coming from. He returned from that raid with no holes or damage and laughing his head off. He told us that they had found a load of aircrew, buzzing around several kites. He gave them one sharp burst that got them running for the air raid shelters and then, just as they had almost made it to the shelters, he caught the whole lot with gunfire.

On my mess, I had another Scotsman by the name of Jock McGuinness. He was stationed on an *Oerlikon* gun under the bows. We were told on the guns that, if a plane dived out of the sun, to 'let him have it', which Jock duly did. Then this American pilot dived out of the sun in a mock attack. The ship hadn't been informed, so Jock only knew it was a plane, so he let him have it. As luck would have it, the pilot managed to bale out. And so Jock had a symbol of the Yank plane mounted on his gun shield – I reckon he was more proud of that than the Japanese plane he had previously shot down!

We had several American observers on board and they couldn't believe that we had another attack of our own going, only three hours after being under Kamikaze threat. In the same incident, their own carrier, *'USS Yorktown',* had been hit, after which she immediately caught fire and went down with 800 casualties. I found out that she had wooden decks, so it was hardly surprising that the fire took hold so rapidly. Our 'flat-tops' had steel decks, so could certainly take more damage than the Yanks. Mind you, at times our flight deck was so hot, you could have cooked your dinner on it!

Saving the Skipper's pride

Our ship again called into the American base at Manus. We had to get the skipper's gig out - he loved boat sailing. But the following day, he was on his way ashore in the barge when he fouled a blob buoy. The tide was coming in, so the stern was slowly going down. Skip was too proud to ask the Yanks for help, and he knew I was out with the Commander in a launch. We noticed the skipper waving to us, so we went alongside to help. Being a diver, I went over the side in my underpants, where I discovered that the buoy cable was as tight as hell around the screw.

I took a deep breath and managed to get down to the bottom. I found that there was a large weight on the seabed, secured by three small hooks. I got one off and went up for more air. Then I got the second one off and went up for more air. Eventually it was down to unhook the third, then down I went for the last time. I was able to straddle the weight and move it directly below the boat. Now there was just enough slack in the wire to get a loop off the screw. The skipper was 'chuffed to death' and my reward was to be a weekend's leave in Sydney.

And so, after finishing the operations on Honshu and Ishe Kaki, a few ships were assembled and headed back for Sydney. There were large crowds on the jetty, waiting for our arrival, as they had heard we had been walloped. All our bridge was burned and blackened, full of holes, and the deck was to be properly repaired. But we got a great welcome and were in dock for two weeks, getting patched up and taking the opportunity to get our heads down – it was Heaven! I had an AB mate called 'Lofty' Kellett in my Bosun's party, for which WO Eastman was the boss. Lofty was a scream - his favourite song was *'My Yiddisha Mama'.* Coming back to the ship one night, through the local park, I heard his song. In the middle of the park was an ornamental pond with four big turtles, one at each corner. I found Lofty in the middle of the shallow pond up, to his neck in the water and singing to the turtles! He was blind drunk of course, so I dragged him back to the ship.

On another occasion, he went into the canteen, which overhung the water at the end of the jetty. Here he ordered ten pints on a tray. He drank nine of these pints and then poured the last pint into his hat. Then he opened the window and dived into the water, which was covered in rubbish, crude oil and gash from the ship! Now when Lofty was sober, he couldn't swim, but now he swam to the ship. But not to the ordinary gangway, oh no, it had to be the officers' gangway. He came up those lovely scrubbed stairs, dripping with oil, spud peelings, and crap from the reeds. At the top, he saluted and

'Jolly Jack' Dunn

The front page of the Australian Sun, 15th October 1945, showing the arrival of POWs

reported for duty, following which he then reclined in the rattle for three weeks. At that time the cells were full up, so they put him in a place outside the brig, made of hessian, with a Marine standing guard. Lofty was very popular with all the mess members, so we used to make up sandwiches and, on the way to the 'heads', we used to throw the grub over the hessian to him, he lived like a King!

Mail from home

I recall looking forward to what we called the 'fleet train', the ships that arrive full of food, oil and ammo, not forgetting the good old mail from home. We had all of our mail censored by the Padre, so one bright spark wrote, as an invitation to the recipient, and in very tiny writing, to *"look under the stamp"*. The Padre must have steamed the stamp off and underneath were the words, *"You nosey old bastard"*. I don't know if the writer was ever forgiven!

Once when I went down to the mess, following a mail delivery, one of the lads was sat with his head in his hands. I put my hand on his shoulder and asked if he was okay and he just passed me a telegram. His mother, wife and kids had all been killed in the blast of a 'doodle-bug' flying bomb. He was just hanging around in a daze for ages afterwards. What can you say to someone in that predicament? My only gesture was to pass him a tot of grog, but I don't think he even tasted it. Then there was a LS Burrell, who told that he had this lousy feeling that he was going to 'cop it' in the next attack. I told him not to be so bloody silly, but he persisted in asking me to inform his girlfriend in Sydney if anything happened to him. I said okay and passed it off.

The following day we were called to 'action stations', it was the dreaded Kamikazes again. He was on the flight deck manning a pom-pom gun. He put one hand on the edge of the deck and the other on the gun-shield. Then, as the gun swung round under power, he got trapped by his head and died instantly – just a stupid accident. That haunted me for a long time. When next in Sydney, I stood outside his girl's house for ages, I couldn't face it and went to turn away. Then she came out and spotted me. She hadn't heard officially of his death, but told me that he had predicted it to her some time back, it was all very weird.

The war draws to a close

Going through the Philippines, the skipper announced that we were altering course, as a volcanic island had suddenly appeared through an eruption. It was already quite large and brown in colour, about two miles long and twenty feet high, with birds already making their homes on it. We were only about sixty miles from the main island of Japan when we received a message that all aircraft were to be grounded, no flights at all. We saw a couple of 'Super Forts' (American heavy bombers) go over and, just afterwards, our Met Officer said he did not know if it was an earthquake or just a tremor, but his instruments had gone mad. Nothing came out on the attack and, even as we edged to within five miles of Japan, there was still no sign of their kites coming at us. We cruised backwards and forwards near the coastline and we could see people on land through

The Australian 8th Division return on HMS Formidable

our strong binoculars. The following morning, the *Tannoy* announced that Japan had surrendered. *(One cannot now ask Jack whether he knew then that the 'earthquake' was caused by an atomic bomb. But it is safe to assume that the American bombers were on their way to either Hiroshima or Nagasaki. Ed.)* It was a weird feeling, we all just looked at one another and thought, *"What do we do now?"* Then the message came through – *"Stand by to go into Tokyo Bay"*.

But in fact we were ordered back to Sydney for repairs, after which we would finally head off to pick up some POWs. We again got a great reception as we sailed into Sydney Harbour, but we were soon heading back out for Java to pick up some Aussies and a few Limeys. They were pretty gaunt looking lads, but were ever so glad to see us, my word. We had prepared the forward mess-decks for them, they slept in the hanger.

Our cooks brewed up some fantastic soup as 'starters' for them, it even had whole chicken legs floating in it. But they hardly touched it. I later queried this with some of the lads and they apologised, saying that they had been practically living on soup, made with either birds, frogs or even snakes, anything in fact that was going! So it was understandable that they couldn't face any more soup. A few of us volunteered to wash up and do all the clearing up. Some of the prisoners told us that, when they had food parcels dropped from aircraft, after hostilities had finished, some had actually died of eating, as their stomachs had shrunk so much, they could not take the large food input. It's hard to believe that chocolate could do so much damage.

Some prisoners' tales

When they came aboard, many of them had to be helped up the gangway. Although they had been released a fortnight previously, many were still suffering with beriberi, dysentery, worms, ulcers and severe malnutrition, I am afraid I have never forgiven those Japs - although the Germans were just as bad! One big chap came aboard, carrying another on his back, who had no legs below his knees. He told me the story that he had been caught smoking, so the guards beat him up, he could hardly stand. Two days later, they caught him again and, needless to say - another beating followed. A week later, the same thing happened again. This time they took him outside, fully bound. They made him kneel on two sharpened bamboo stakes with a cord tied around his neck, then round the branch of a tree and finally to the ring-pull of a hand grenade. It was also snowing. The poor devil stuck it for over twenty hours until he finally collapsed.

It turned out that the grenade was only a dummy. The victim's legs went gangrenous, their own Japanese doctor operated to save his life. He amputated both legs with a steak knife and a saw from the kitchen, then cauterised the stumps with a red-hot tablespoon. The chap actually got through it, but God knows how! Our shipwrights scrounged a chrome chair from the wardroom and made a wheelchair for him, he went up and down the flight deck like a rocket.

His friendly carrier was lost without the burden, after all he had carried him for the previous two years. I wrote to both of them for about ten years afterwards, as one was called William Thomas Dunn, while my brother's name was Thomas William Dunn. And then all of a sudden - no more letters. Whether or not they had 'snuffed it', nobody knows. My son-in-law once went out to Melbourne with his job. He asked the lady in the office if she could help, as I had the address of the lad with the same name as mine – 'Dunn'. When my son-in-law came back home, it was with a big grin on his face and a whole list of people called Dunn. I nearly died, there were about five thousand names, so I had to give up.

There were quite a few English lads amongst those POWs, their names were posted on the end of their beds. So I went down to the hanger to check if there was anyone from Hampshire or Sussex. I got to this one bed, its occupant had a shaved head and weighed about six stone, soaking wet, looking a lot like Mahatma Gandhi. He looked up and, all of a sudden, he jumped off the bed and grabbed me. I thought to myself, *"Who the hell are you?" "Don't you know me Jack?"* he cried. I made out that I could not remember his name. *"I used to load your lorry Jack!"* came the startling response.

It turned out that he was a brick loader from Midhurst brickyard and it all came back to me. But how could you hope to recognise any poor soul in that state? Most of them had been used as slave labour on the Burma Railway. Two years after I was demobbed and I still used to go to his pub once a year. He used to spot me and it was a bit embarrassing really, as he used to tell everyone, *"This here is the man that brought me back from the Japs"*. The following year he was run over outside the pub, he never even married. What a sad way to finish.

The POWs used to love the deck hockey we used to play. When we got near to Sydney, the Aussies were all dressed in their jungle green, slouch hats and all, fell in on the flight deck. As we came into the harbour, hundreds of boats came out to meet us, they had all kinds of names on their sides. All of a sudden, as much-loved families were spotted, off came the boots, hats and shirts. Loads of them dived off the flight deck, from a height of about forty feet, and it was great to see Mums and Dads, wives and sweethearts, relatives near and dear, all crying with joy. Some may say that there is no God, but Sydney Harbour is well known for sharks, and for all the lads that dived in, not one was taken, so somebody was looking down, even if it wasn't obvious at all times! When we got alongside, the invites we received were amazing – I'd still be out there now if I'd accepted them all.

The Indians

Our next job was picking up some Indian POWs. At least they looked a darn sight better than the Aussies, perhaps they were better suited to surviving on meagre rations.

The welcome sight of Sydney Harbour bridge

There were Punjabis, Sikhs and many more. We showed them to the toilets but most of them didn't use toilet paper, they took their drinking vessels and washed themselves. I suppose really it's cleaner than us, but they stood on the seats, so the toilets were awash! A lot of them used to sleep on the flight deck. One of the laughs was, when it was time for their prayers at sunset, they couldn't make out the direction where Mecca was – they were stumped. So the skipper made a signpost with all their dialects on and set it up in the middle of the flight deck. So every time the ship altered course, a rating used to come down from the bridge and alter the sign! One thing that used to make me shudder was when the Indians used to shave. They had their own barbers and used to 'dry shave'. It used to give me a shiver right up my back to hear the rasping noise. They once offered to give me a shave, but no way!

I used to talk with one Punjabi soldier as he lay on his bed, in a pretty bad state. He was so thin, he could not eat solids, just liquids, and he told me that he was dying. He was well educated, all he wanted was to see India one last time before he died. As we got close to Bombay, we smelt India long before we saw it, as there was loads of rubbish floating past us. As we came alongside in Bombay, an Indian Pipe Band was playing, they were brilliant. Just as we touched shore, the poor Punjabi died, it must have been only his sheer willpower that had kept him going. When we first took the Indians on board, we had some lovely cutlery, all chrome spoons, ladles and all the utensils. They started using them at first but, when we returned half an hour later, they were sat cross-legged on the counters with their 'nosh' in bowls and they were dishing out the food by the handful, it was very humourous.

Those Indians were dead keen on the old curry, I even used to see them eat the curry powder dry. We made a lovely servery for them on the forward mess-deck. There was chrome servers, scoops, forks and ladles. We went back half an hour later and their cooks were sat on the servery with the Dixies between their legs, dishing the grub out with their bare hands. At night, they used to do native dances. They would form a circle with bamboo sticks in their hands and just two small drums to get their rhythm going, going around in a ring and getting faster and faster until they all dropped down exhausted and covered in sweat. Lofty and I got up and started doing the hula-hula dance, I could always wiggle my rear, they loved it and wouldn't let us stop, so that in the end I was absolutely knackered! We all fought – and danced - for the same Empire.

After a few days shore leave, it really shook you when you saw the poverty in the streets. Little children deliberately crippled, just for the purpose of begging. The trams and trains were amazing, I've never seen so many people hanging on to the outsides of vehicles. A native came up to us and asked if we would like to see a fight between snakes and a mongoose. Being matelots, we are suckers for anything different. We all gathered around this guy, and he tipped out a snake about four feet long and then the mongoose. The snake started to strike at the mongoose, which was so quick, just like a bit of silk. It struck four times, then all of a sudden it wavered one way. The mongoose was in like a flash, there was a crunch, and the snake's head was gone. The snake-man then tipped out another big snake, followed by a very small one. He called it a bamboo snake and it was like greased lightning. It was, he said, the deadliest snake in India and the bigger snake died in a few minutes.

The snake man had snakebites all up his arms. A little boy kept pulling the snakes back into the ring - I had a position to make a quick getaway! Another Indian came and asked if I had a gold ring, which I hadn't, but my chum had one. The Indian said he could put 'The Lord's Prayer' on the ring for two rupees. So I stood behind him. He got a block of lead out of his pocket, with a slit to fit the ring. It was dark, so he sat on his rear on the pavement, under a gaslight. I couldn't see the ring in the poor light, but in twenty minutes he done a perfect job. Other craftsmen were sat in alcoves about three foot by four, they held the brass plates with their feet and worked with both hands and no electric light. But their work was perfect. I made sure I never had any loose change to take back to the ship - I was a bit wary about 'con artists'!

This well dressed young Indian had once caught me a treat. He stopped me and said, *"You have a lucky face and I will tell your fortune"*. He asked me to put a few *annas* (Indian money) in his hand and then gave me a few facts that were very true. Then he said that, if I put a *rupee* (another Indian coin) in his hand, he had something to my interest. Muggins coughed up and he was away up the street like Jesse Owens! You live and learn. Little boys were sent out to pull in sailors on the way home, as they knew you are out looking for presents. This one little lad got hold of my hand and he had such a nice little face, only about six years old. He might well have been the only breadwinner in the house, as poverty was everywhere. It was a laugh going back to the ship, with chaps carrying all sorts - carpets, suitcases, handbags. When I got back aboard, one of the lads asked where I had got my filigree brooch, as he wanted a suitcase. So I took him the day afterwards.

The same little lad was outside the dockyard gate. He saw me coming and caught hold of my hand. We were taken to the same shop, where the owner started off with a price about four quid. *"Too dear"* was my answer - if you give them the full price, they break their heart that they did not charge more! You have to bargain, it's the custom. The next price quoted was three quid, plus five *Woodbines*. We finished up at two pounds ten shillings and two cigarettes. The suitcase was pure leather with strong straps. The little boy was given a few annas for his help. As we were leaving the ship, the owner was going around with a smoking candle, so I asked him in a polite manner what was the reason? He told me that it was to keep away evil spirits away on closing - little did he know that the evil spirits were just leaving!

When the Indian ex-prisoners had left the ship, we could still smell the aroma of curry wherever we went. They took over the Petty Officers' (POs') toilets, taking their drinking vessels with them when they 'did their business'. This was so they could wash themselves clean – no rubbing it until you lose it for them – far more hygienic! When the POs got their quarters back, they stunk of curry as well, so we then had a curry-flavoured ship for a long time afterwards.

Our next job was to take a section of Gurkhas to Java, as the Dutch inhabitants were

Christmas 1945 and ready to go home at last

getting a lot of trouble from the locals. We then returned to Sydney and had to march in the Victory Parade. My God, that march was about three miles and, with rifles held 'at the slope', it was murder. They were throwing ticker tape out of the office windows, it was wrapping around our legs and we could hardly walk, but they certainly gave us a hell of a reception. So we had our repairs done, patches all over the bridge and island, then we said our farewells to a great country.

On the way back we came around the Cape and had a few days in Cape Town. I had been there before, it was a marvellous run ashore. We enjoyed a visit to a hotel in Cape Town, as 'Lofty' Kellett had a brother who ran the place. He knew we were on the way home, so he gave Lofty a full smoked gammon, to take home to his mother. Lofty hung it in my Bosun's store and the smell was gorgeous. He suggested a slice each so we unscrewed the heater off the bulkhead, laid it flat and cooked the gammon slices with fried bread. The aroma drifted all around the fo'castle and made your mouth water. We had several slices on the way home as, whenever he asked if I fancied a bacon butty, I just couldn't say no. So, when we finally arrived, we only had a two-pound piece of bacon left - including the bone!

Back home – to a hero's welcome

Heading north, the temperature started dropping, but we were warmed up by the sight of Southsea Castle. We came into Pompey with a 350-foot 'paying-off' pennant streaming out behind us. The then girlfriend – or should I say fiancée? - was on the jetty with my Mum and Dad. The gangway was put down and they all came aboard. My future wife Brenda had got onto the wrong train and had been on the way to Brighton, but she managed to get to the dock with my Mum and Dad in time. They had to come through the hanger, as there were half-naked blokes all over the place, getting ready to go ashore - but nobody seemed to bother.

Lofty was alongside me with his part gammon and he had bought his Mum a set of glamourous black underwear, just like a film star's, which would have fitted a girl of eighteen. His Mum was about sixteen stone and wouldn't have got even one leg into it – but that was Lofty for you! We were then sent to Stamshaw Camp, Cosham, and two days later we were demobbed. I dropped the outfitter ten bob (fifty pence in today's money!) and he fitted me up with a nice clerical grey suit, shirt and raincoat, shinny shoes and a pork pie hat. It was the first suit I had ever owned. Then it was off home with Mum, Dad and Bren.

I arrived at Liss Station, having been away for some two years, when a chap called Fred Watts, who was in the Liss Fire Brigade, spotted me and shouted, *"Home again then, Jack?"* I could have choked him, as I'd been away for two years and he'd never even been out of Liss – still, that's life. Then it was on the Liss & District bus to **Greatham** and home, where the banners were out – *"Welcome home"* - it was all a bit embarrassing.

My Dad asked me, *"How did you get on son?"* I thought I would put one over on him, knowing that he had once served in Egypt. I told him that I had to patrol the brothels in 'Alex' and, on checking one of them, I told him that the old Madam who ran the place asked me where I came from. I told her that I was from England and that my father had served in Egypt many years ago. She then said, *"I knew an English soldier that was in the REs, his name was Tommy Dunn"*. The look on my Dad's face was one of shock, but his instant reply was, *"Don't go telling your mother about this"*. He must have known I was only leg pulling.

The final crack was that I got my medals, two more than Dad, but he told me that I'd earned mine! I answered, *"Where do you think I got them from, off a Colman's mustard tin?"* He was really proud of me, but I had to have my joke, I had waited a long time. But after all we went through it still makes you wonder who won the bloody war, there is still fighting all over the world. So there I Dunn, signing off, with no hammock to sling and back to civvie-street and a demob suit. Before I had gone into the Navy, I had joined the Home Guard at the tender age of sixteen. I was provided with a broom handle with a bayonet tied on one end and told that if a paratrooper came down, I was to run out and hold the bayonet under his backside! Why should Britain tremble, eh?

Looking back now, I was lucky to get home after some near misses. My worst time was when I fell off the bottom of the old ship, while cleaning an inlet valve. They say that if you drop more than thirty feet, your body is pushed up into your helmet! I hit the bottom of Sydney Harbour, which thankfully was only ten feet from the bottom of the ship. Your life certainly flashes before you in a second at times like that. But I have never regretted volunteering, you don't know how ignorant you are about how the rest of the world survives. You go to war as a boy and come back a man.

Civvie Street

I had a week's holiday and then realised that I had to earn my keep. So I went back to my old firm, driving heavy lorries, luckily they took me on straight away. But the trucks were in a hell of a state, as any good motor at the start of the war had been taken over by the Army. The brakes weren't all that good so I used to put my trust in the Lord and keep my bowels open. I was still courting Bren and eventually, in 1947, I asked her if she could put up with me for life. She said *"Yes"*, she must have thought I had money, Ha-ha, joke!

We were married at Wymering Church and it was definitely the best move I ever made. It has now lasted nearly sixty years, we have two great kids, with grandchildren and great-grandchildren. We tied the knot in the month of March, so we got a bit of tax back, the grand sum of £24. We were actually married on a total of seventy quid, my reward for serving King and country. Life was pretty hard, but we managed to get a two-up and two-down cottage, no drains and no sanitation. I had spent most of my life in Army quarters, so I wasn't used to having a bucket to empty every week and nor was Bren. Then it started getting really modern - they sent a lorry around to empty the bucket. You can't stop progress! Ha-ha! I will now sign off, as Sunday dinner has arrived!

From an old ex-matelot, PJX 298263.

(Jack Dunn wrote the final words above on the Sunday before he was taken into hospital. Brenda later told me that she swears Jack had a premonition that those words would be his last attempt at writing. Ed.)

'Jolly Jack' Dunn

Wedding Day March 1947

'Jolly Jack' Dunn

Greatham Church

'Jolly Jack' Dunn

Life in post-war Greatham

Everyone in those days was on rations - food, blankets and furniture. Our bedside cabinets were just orange boxes with curtains across them. The house was so very cold in the winter, we even used to put the carpet on the bed as well. I remember that one night the bed went down at one end. We had gone through the worm-eaten floor and the legs were sticking through the kitchen ceiling. If you had the money, you could buy those items you needed, as most things were issued on dockets. In 1947, my wage was £3 and ten shillings a week. We didn't get much meat a week, so Bren used to give me extra potatoes and veg to fill me up. I used to carry a pellet gun with me on the lorry - I will admit that I was something of a poacher, but only to help out with the food shortage.

It was two years before we had our daughter Jennifer. When she started teething, it was hell, she would cry all night. I used to go to work in a dream. I used to pick Bren up in the lorry, along with Jennifer, and she used to sleep all day with the motion – but then howl all night. My lorry was pretty rough though, as at times you could not stop very quickly when fully loaded. I told Bren *"If I say jump - jump!"* It certainly taught you how to drive! Two years later we had John, who was totally different - he would sleep all through the night.

We had many amusing situations at work. One of our drivers, George Webb, had just come out of the RAF, so he used to wear his old battle dress for work. One job was to take lime to this chicken farm and spread it in the chicken runs, to sweeten the ground. We took the sheet off the load and hung it over the wire netting. Inside the run were several sheep and a ram, which kept butting the folded sheet. I said to George that rams were allergic to the colour blue. So if he put his behind to the wire netting, the ram would back away. He said, *"You're pulling my leg!"* I told him, *"Okay then, try it and I'll prove it is true"*.

George put his rear end to the wire, then looked back and saw the ram backing away. I started to speak to George and, of course, he looked back at me. At that point the ram put his head down and charged. It hit George dead on target, knocking him straight across the road, and he hit the chicken run opposite. The wire bent over and then flicked back up, George did a complete somersault into the muck run. He got up and then chased me round the chicken farm with his shovel. I am sure he would have crowned me if he'd caught me, Ha-ha. Even now, at over ninety years of age, old George still has a laugh about it.

We were then given some German POWs to help us, some were from the *'Volksturm'*, their Home Guard. I remember that one of them was only four foot six. They were great lads, they hadn't wanted to fight any more than we did, and it turned out that they were very good workers. Another time, I had a Romany lad called Jim as a driver's mate. He used to back up the lorry under a big chute to load up with lime. Sometimes, the live lime used to stick in the chute, so he had to go up and poke the lime to start it flowing again. All of a sudden, there was a hell of a rush of lime and he came through the chute as well. I filled the lorry dead level in about two seconds, when up through the lime appeared Jim, still with his trilby on and looking like *'Snow White'*. His eyes, ears and nose were full of lime. I lifted him off and washed him off in a rainwater tank, he was really shook up. But it had been a comical sight to see him rising to the surface through the lime!

I had another mate, who we called 'Yorkie', his surname was Spenceley. He was very fond of sparring about, flicking your nose with his hand. But on this particular day, as he put out his arm, I snatched him to my chest. Now, I'm fifty-odd inches around the chest and I have always been strong in the arms, so as I gave him a squeeze, he went out like a light. I had scary visions of the noose, hanging on the end of its rope - I thought I had killed him. I managed to get some water out of a ditch and bathed his face. It took twenty minutes to bring him round, but he didn't spar any more after that.

As mentioned previously, those lorries were in a hell of a state. One I had the misfortune to drive literally used to drink oil. There was a long slope from Midhurst up to Redford and, when we were fully loaded, my young mate used to stand on the front bumper and pour a gallon of oil into the engine while we were still under way. You couldn't do that nowadays, with all the traffic. In fact, the wagons wouldn't even be on the road today, with the MoT regulations. There was one day, when I was going down a country lane loaded with lime, that I came to a hairpin bend with a farmyard right on the corner. The steering went completely and I ran into the five-barred gate head on. The gate flew open and I hit a very large heap of cow manure, about thirty or forty tons of it. The stuff went in all directions and drove the engine back into the cab. I shot forward into the windscreen, but got away with just a bump. That was the end of that old heap.

Another job I had to do was to take one of those old 1928 bull-nosed *Morris* vans to *Smiths'* clock factory, to deliver a load of electric coils. There was no foot brake at all and only the merest fraction of a handbrake. I would put the seat as close as I could to the steering wheel so that, when I went across London, I would have one hand on the handbrake, signal with my right arm and steer a straight line with my stomach - it was certainly an adventure! You'd never do it nowadays, the way the traffic is.

Working at Longmoor Camp

Eventually, the transport business got a bit dodgy, so I got a job in the Longmoor Garrison Engineers' yard, doing maintenance on the married quarters and the Army Camp. I had a year during which I worked on plumbing, but then they ran short of money and, instead, I then got a job at the NAAFI store and shop. Mr Seaton was the manager and I got made up to charge-hand. We used to supply the local units with their rations, as well as all the Officers' and Sergeants' Messes. We had one officers' wife who had been in India for many years. She would try and knock you down on the price of the fruit, as she used to make a lot of jam. When I used to see her coming, I would put up the price of the plums by tuppence (two old pennies) a pound. I would then tell her that, if she took seven pounds at a time, I would take tuppence a pound off. I would win every time, Ha-ha.

An aerial view of Greatham Village, circa 2000

If one of the girls served her (it was all counter service in those days), then she would ask for half-a-pound of *Rover* assorted biscuits. The girl would give her a half-pound packet but she would refuse them, saying that she wanted loose biscuits. She would then add, *"Jack knows what I have"*. They used to shout at me to come into the shop. I would see her and say, *"Good morning Mrs McDonald, you want your usual biscuits?"* *"Yes please, Jack"*, she'd reply. I would then go out into the back, undo a packet of *Rover*, and pour them into a bag. Then I'd march back into the shop and weigh them up, chip in with a *"Thank you madam"*, and off she'd go, as happy as Larry! She'd occasionally ask me *"Why don't the girls serve me loose ones?"* but my reply means that I'll never go to heaven.

We used to get the Army Reserves every year for a fortnight's camp. They used to put officers in charge of the Mess, but they didn't know very much about the job, so we used to help them a lot, especially when the GOC's visit was due – that's the General Officer Commanding. One young officer came down in a panic, so it was a case of *"Jack, can you help?"* He had forgotten the flowers for the centre of the table and was terrified. I told him not to worry, then went home and picked a load of dahlia heads. We had no vases, so I told him to put the heads down the centre of the table, at which he asked, *"Are you sure?"* But he did as he was told and earned himself a hell of a pat on the back from the General!

One officer used to ask for things that he thought I knew nothing about. I overheard him tell his subaltern that he wanted some *Port Salut* cheese served at the next function. I quickly got my book out, before he came in, the bigheaded sod. He said to me, *"I don't suppose you know what Port Salut cheese is, do you Jack?"* to which I replied, *"Oh yes. It's a special cheese made by Trappist Monks in Northern France"*. He was amazed at that, while the young subaltern was tickled to death, he used to laugh every time he came in. The bumptious officer never tried it again after that.

Another laugh came when I used to go around the officers' married quarters to take their orders. Major Higgins' wife used to say, *"Come in Jack, I'm in bed, just come up!"* It was a bit embarrassing, she had no shame, and I had to tell myself, *"You are a married man, Jack"*. Talk about opportunity knocks! A few days later, she came into the shop and the manager mentioned that her monthly account was overdue. She turned around to me and said. *"Jack, are you going around with the order?" "Yes"*, I replied. To which she then said, *"Well, will you go upstairs in my house and get my cheque book. It's near where you normally sit when you take my order"*. Was I blushing! The manager asked, *"What the hell do you get up to?"* but he knew what she was like.

Another officer's wife used to come in and ask one of the girls for bacon. The girl would weigh it up and then the lady would then say, *"That's not my usual bacon, get Jack, he knows"*. So I used to take the bacon out the back, turn it over on the greaseproof paper, then go back into the shop and show it to the lady in question. She would then remark, *"Why can't that girl serve me like that?"* Then she'd head off home happy.

Becoming a butcher

I then changed jobs, going to work as a butcher at Bordon. What a job that was, from 5.30 in the morning until 6 o'clock at night, with deliveries to be made all around the camp. But there were quite a few laughs on that job too. I delivered a chicken to one Army quarter and the lady who answered the door was very attractive, standing there in a flesh-coloured bikini. I was quite taken aback, as she was blonde and just like a *'Page Three'* girl. Now when I used to take their orders, I would ask if they wanted sage and onion stuffing. If they said, *"Yes please"*, I would write 'S/O' on their order. But now, with the shock of seeing her state of dress, I forgot all about the stuffing.

I'd just got back to my van when a load of Army lads went doubling past on PT. Our pin-up came out into the rain in her bikini and shouted across, *"Jack, I wanted stuffing as well!"* Oh my god, for the next six months, wherever I was, all around the Camp, any lads on PT used to shout, *"Hey butcher, we want stuffing"*. She probably didn't realise what she had said at the time, but she also pulled my leg for weeks afterwards.

I also used to deliver to the caravan site, where this one woman had ordered pig's liver. I knocked at the door and a voice said, *"Come in"*. What a shock! I went into the van and she was stood there, stark naked, in the bath. I twisted around to leave and found that my fifty-odd inch chest was jammed in the caravan doors, which were very narrow. I struggled through and literally fell out into a bed of flowers, with the liver sliding all over me. What a life!

After ten years in that job, the Bordon butcher sold up, so I went to work for the *Gateways Supermarket* down in Petersfield. That was another place for laughs. One lady was the widow of a Naval Commander, who had gone down with his ship. I used to bring up things in conversation to try and cheer her up. This one time I mentioned that it was quite a feat to bring up the *'Mary Rose'*. (That was the flagship of King Henry VIII, which sank in 1545, then raised from the seabed of the Solent off Southsea in 1982. Personally, I thought it was a waste of money.) Her next comment was, *"Butcher, were you on the 'Mary Rose'?"* My young butcher's boy laughed his head off. I replied, *"Madam, I wasn't very familiar with Henry the Eighth!"* She then thought about it for a minute and asked, *"I suppose that is what they call a Navy clanger?"* It was several months before that topic died down.

Another good laugh - a lady used to come in that owned *'Tiger Toys'*. She never liked waiting. She was on the bacon counter one day and I was serving about six people on the butchery. She shouted across, *"Butcher, have you got chicken legs?"* I couldn't resist the swift riposte, *"Madam, my legs have gone that shape running backwards and forwards behind this block"*. She never came in any more, thank goodness. One day, I was trying to deal with half a dozen people waiting to be served, when Bren came into the shop, marched up to the front of the queue and asked me what time I'd be home. One lady customer said, *"Take your turn"*, even though Bren had only asked a question. Being a leg-puller, I just said to the lady, *"It's OK madam, it's just the woman I sleep with"*. She never cottoned on for about six months that it was a wind-up, she continued to give my wife dirty looks.

At that time we had a meat supervisor who had no time for older butchers. He came in one day, bragging that he had just got rid of a butchery manager of sixty years old. Not long after that, he started on me. I got so wound up that I chucked in the manager's job and got transferred to the Liphook branch, where I worked right up until I was sixty-eight. They gave me a great send off when I finally retired, about fifty of my old bosses and staff. So both Bren and I now work in a Charity shop for half a day each week. It's great seeing a lot of my old customers, apart from picking up a lot of bargains.

I really think we should get a Red Cross for my car, as I regularly visit an old Navy chum who is very ill with angina and stone trouble. Another chum of mine is dying of cancer - I supply him every week with videos. Yet another old pal suffers with severe depression, another one has had a bad heart attack, while an old mate of ninety years old has just gone into a home.

I still dress up as Father Xmas every year for the Bordon children, then for the local old peoples' home. Another two days I entertain for the kindergarten up at the School. There are so many tasks I do over two days, such as Saturday for the Heart Foundation Xmas Party and Sunday it's the Xmas dinner at the *'Country Market'* complex up at Bordon.

(I have added Jack's account of post-war life at the end of his story about service with the Royal Navy. With his childhood memories at the very beginning, the whole of Jack's life, as recounted by the man himself, is now laid out above. Ed.)

www.ingramcontent.com/pod-product-compliance
Ingram Content Group UK Ltd.
Pitfield, Milton Keynes, MK11 3LW, UK
UKHW041433180426
11947UKWH00007B/415